Ada Byron Lovelace

and the

Thinking Machine

By
Laurie Wallmark

Illustrated By
April Chu

Creston Books

Ada was born into a world of poetry, but numbers, not words, captured her imagination.

Her mother, Lady Byron, had a passion for geometry. In fact, her nickname was "The Princess of Parallelograms."

But her famous father dominated the household. Beloved for his Romantic poems, Lord Byron was a celebrity throughout the world.

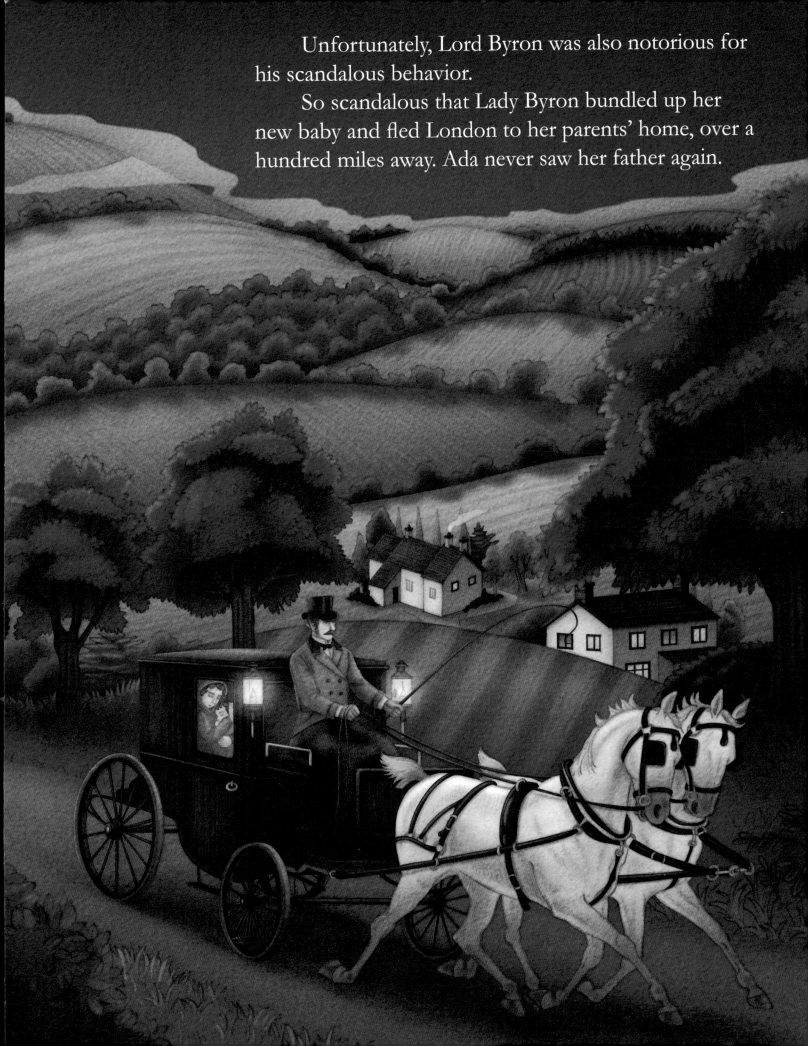

Unfortunately, Lord Byron was also notorious for his scandalous behavior.

So scandalous that Lady Byron bundled up her new baby and fled London to her parents' home, over a hundred miles away. Ada never saw her father again.

Now Ada could only know her father through his books. And with her mother often traveling, Ada was lonely. Her journals, filled with pages of inventions and equations, kept her company.

The best part was when her sketches flew off the page and became real.

Ada's latest invention was a flying machine. She had built a set of real wings, but could they actually fly? First, Ada needed to compute the wings' power. She broke the problem into steps — surface area and weight, wind speed and angles. Multiplying and dividing, over and over again. Ada loved numbers, but these calculations seemed endless. Wasn't there an easier way? Writing for so long made her fingers hurt. She wriggled them and returned to her numbers. Fifteen times twelve equals one hundred and eighty...

The sky darkened and thunder
crashed. Rain pounded on the roof
and pelted through the open window.
Ada jumped up to latch the shutters. The
curtains flapped in and out, like sails billowing
in the wind.

Sails! Sails were like wings! Ada could use this
wind to do an experiment for her flying machine. She
grabbed her journal and charged out into the howling storm.

Again and again Ada launched her model sailboat across the pond. Each time, she adjusted the sails and studied the effect on the little boat's speed. A storm of numbers and calculations whirled in her mind and spilled onto her pages.

Night fell. Ada returned home — muddy, dripping wet, and triumphant.

When Nanny saw Ada, she scolded her for being out in such dreadful weather. She sniffed that she didn't care what Lady Byron thought. Girls should not waste their time with math and science and experiments and other such nonsense. But to Ada, it wasn't nonsense at all. Numbers were her friends.

After dinner, she sprawled on the floor with her puzzle book. Her head was hot and achy. The numbers squirmed about on the paper, and her eyes felt as if they were filled with sand from the pond.

By morning, Ada had a high fever. Nanny didn't scold now. She was worried. She cabled Mama to come home right away. Ada had the measles.

Through many long days and nights, Mama read Ada her favorite books. The fever finally broke, but the measles left her paralyzed and blind.

To keep Ada's mind sharp, Mama quizzed her on math problems. How much was eighty-two minus twenty-five? Eighteen times forty-seven? Ninety-six divided by thirteen? Numbers chased each other around and around in Ada's head.

Mama posed ever harder problems, and Ada solved them all. Problems like how long does it take to travel to London? By carriage, it was an overnight journey. But Ada's flying machine could go much faster than a carriage. If Ada flew, she'd be able to reach London in only a few hours. Just in time for tea!

Ada's numbers kept her company. Fifteen times twelve was still one hundred and eighty and always would be, whether Ada could see or not.

Over the next few weeks, her eyes got better, but it was three long years before she could put away her crutches. The girl who wanted to fly could not even walk.

But Ada still had her numbers. Numbers that mattered to her more than ever.

Mama recognized her daughter's passion. She hired tutors so Ada could learn math at an even higher level. Ada's favorite was Mary Fairfax Somerville, the well-known scientist and mathematician.

Somerville was living proof that girls could do math and do it well. She had even written books on the subject, another thing girls were not supposed to do.

Somerville was so impressed by Ada's sharp reasoning skills, she invited Ada and her mother to a party. Not just a party for dancing and dining, but for sharing ideas. The guests were scientists like Michael Faraday, who studied electromagnetism, and Charles Wheatstone, who invented a device to display three-dimensional images.

But for Ada, the one who mattered most was Charles Babbage. He was a famous mathematician and inventor, just like Ada wanted to be. Though she was only seventeen and Babbage forty-one, Ada spoke about math with a precision and understanding that impressed him. So much so, that Babbage invited her to visit his laboratory.

Ada brought her journals to show him her own experiments and inventions. Their tea grew cold as they talked about their love of machines and mathematics. Babbage didn't see her as simply a young girl. He treated her like the fellow mathematician and inventor she already was.

Before, numbers had been Ada's only friends. Now Babbage was a friend as well.

Babbage showed Ada his Difference Engine,
a revolutionary mechanical calculator. He knew
Ada would understand how his extraordinary
invention worked.

Ada did more than understand. She couldn't wait to see the Difference Engine in action. She chose to have the machine solve a simple problem, one she could easily do in her head. Fifteen times twelve.

Reaching inside the machine, Ada rotated the metal columns until the numbers 15 and 12 appeared. With a crank of the handle, she powered the calculator.

Gears clicked and turned. Cylinders pumped up and down. Small hammers clanked as the numbers spiraled upward, guiding the machine to the correct solution. After a few turns of the handle, the answer appeared on the final column — 180. It was right!

Babbage told Ada he had designed an even more powerful device, a mechanical computer. His Analytical Engine would solve harder problems by working through them step by step. It could even make decisions all by itself, a true thinking machine.

The only trouble was, Babbage hadn't actually built it.

Analytical Engine

Analytical Engine

output

input

mill

if x, then y

weaving
algebraic
patterns

PROBABILITY

JACOB BERNOULLI

Ada carried home a stack of Babbage's lab books, thirty in all, filled with his notes about the Analytical Engine. Back in her room, she studied the technical descriptions and pored over the diagrams.

Ada quickly realized that without instructions, the Analytical Engine would be a useless pile of metal parts. It needed numbers to make it work.

Her numbers.

Her friends!

Ada decided to create an algorithm, a set of mathematical instructions, for the Analytical Engine. The machine could follow these instructions and solve a complex math problem, one difficult to figure out by hand.

She worked for months revising her instructions. Countless lines of numbers and symbols poured onto her journal pages.

After checking and rechecking her algorithm through the night, Ada finally laid down her pen. She hadn't found any errors. The world's first computer program was complete.

The gears of Ada's mind whirred with possibilities for future inventions, all controlled by computing machines.

She imagined computers would someday design powerful flying machines and majestic sailing ships. They would draw pictures and compose music. And they would play games and help with schoolwork.

Because Babbage never finished building the Analytical Engine, Ada never got to see her program run. But the influence of her work lives on. More than one hundred years before the invention of the modern computer, Ada had glimpsed the future and had created a new profession — computer programming.

Ada couldn't know that one day a computer language would be named after her — *Ada*. And one of *Ada's* uses? To guide modern flying machines.

The girl who needed crutches ended up flying after all!

Author's Note

As a child, Ada loved making mechanical toys and gadgets, like her flying machines and model sailboats. In a letter to the well-known mathematician Mary Fairfax Somerville, she described her passionate interest:

> I am afraid that when a machine, or a lecture, or anything of the kind,
> comes my way, I have no regard for time, space, or any ordinary obstacles.[1]

To further Ada's studies, Lady Byron hired professional mathematicians as tutors, including Somerville, William Frend, Dr. William King, and Augustus De Morgan.

Somerville in turn introduced Ada to Charles Babbage, the famous mathematician and inventor. Ada and Babbage met often to discuss math and science. In time, Ada understood as much, if not more, than Babbage did about his inventions.

She was thrilled to read an article written by Luigi Menabrea about Babbage's latest machine, the Analytical Engine. Because of Ada's superior mathematical and language skills, Babbage asked her to translate the article from French to English. Ada soon realized Menabrea's explanation was incomplete, and she had the expertise needed to provide the missing technical details.

With Babbage's encouragement, Ada added this information as notes to the translation. Her additions turned out to be about twice as long as the original article. These notes included her design of the world's first computer program.

When Ada's notes were published, her name didn't appear on them. Instead, as was common for that era, she hid her gender by signing only her initials, "A.A.L.," instead of her full name, Augusta Ada Lovelace. During her lifetime, the public never knew this ground-breaking work had been written by a woman.

Ada predicted many possible uses for computing machines. While her ideas then sounded like science fiction, over one hundred and fifty years later, all of her amazing predictions have come true.

Ada realized the possibilities for computers were almost limitless. But they needed a human mind to give them instructions. In her Note G added to Menabrea's article, Ada wrote:

> The Analytical Engine has no pretension whatever to *originate* any thing.
> It can do whatever *we know how to order it* to perform. It can *follow* analysis;
> but it has no power of *anticipating* any analytical relations or truths.[2]

Unfortunately, society and circumstances made it difficult for Ada to live the life she'd dreamed of, that of a professional mathematician. This didn't stop her from pursuing her interest in math and science. In a letter to August De Morgan, she wrote:

> I am never really satisfied that I understand *anything*, because,
> understand it as well as I may, my comprehension *can* only be
> an infinitesimal fraction of all I want to understand.[3]

Ada never stopped learning. She enjoyed the intellectual challenge of writing about scientific topics such as electricity, magnetism, and biology. She proposed using math to understand how the brain creates thoughts, a "calculus of the nervous system." Her journals overflowed with mathematical theories, exercises, and puzzles.

Ada's legacy lives on in programming today. Every October, people around the world observe Ada Lovelace Day (www.findingada.com), a holiday to celebrate women in technology. Thousands of Internet bloggers post about the many women who work as computer programmers, engineers, and scientists. Ada would be delighted to know her accomplishments encourage girls to enter the world of computers.

The World's First Computer Program

Programs tell a computer what to do and how to do it. The instructions have to be detailed and precise, since, as Ada remarked, computers can't think for themselves.

Ada's program for the Analytical Engine calculated Bernoulli numbers. These are used to solve difficult problems in advanced mathematics. Without the help of a computer, they are extremely difficult and time-consuming to figure out.

To write the program, Ada designed a mathematical algorithm. This was a detailed plan for finding the solution. First, Ada broke the problem into a series of simple steps. Then she created a thorough list of instructions to carry out these steps. These included which numbers to add, subtract, multiply, or divide. They also told the machine where and how to make decisions.

When modern-day computer scientists tested Ada's software, they found she had made only one minor mistake, which was easily fixed. Ada's program was almost perfect.

Ada's Nicknames

Bride of Science: As a teenager, Ada gave herself this name to show her desire to devote her life to math and science instead of simply being a wife and mother, the only roles most women held at the time.
Carrier Pigeon: Ada signed letters to Mama this way. She called Mama, "Hen."
Enchantress of Numbers: Babbage called Ada this because of her incredible mathematical abilities.
High Priestess of Babbage's Engine: Ada used this fanciful title for herself to show she was the expert on the Analytical Engine, a mechanical computer.

For more educational resources, visit www.crestonbooks.co

[1] Lovelace, Ada. Letter to Mary Somerville. 8 July 1834. MS.

[2] Menabrea, L. F. "Sketch of the Analytical Engine Invented by Charles Babbage, Esq. with Notes by the Translator." Scientific Memoirs 722 (1834). Print.

[3] Lovelace, Ada. Letter to Augustus De Morgan. 6 July 1841. MS.

Timeline

1815 Augusta Ada Byron is born in London, England. (December 10)

1828 Age 12, Ada designs a flying machine.

1829 Age 13, Ada gets measles, leaving her temporarily blind and paralyzed.

1833 Age 17, Ada meets Charles Babbage and studies his Difference Engine.

1835 Age 19, Ada marries William King (later Earl of Lovelace).

1836 Age 20, Ada's son, Byron, is born. Her other children, Annabella and Ralph, soon follow.

1837 Age 21, Ada contracts cholera and is bedridden for months.

1841 Age 25, Ada writes an essay on the use of imagination in creating science.

1843 Age 27, Ada publishes her notes on the Analytical Engine in *Taylor's Scientific Memoirs*. Note G includes the world's first computer program.

1852 Age 36, Lady Ada Byron Lovelace dies of cancer. (November 27)

Partial Bibliography

Baum, Joan. *The Calculating Passion of Ada Byron*. Hamden: Archon Books, 1986.

Essinger, James. *Ada's Algorithm: How Lord Byron's Daughter Ada Lovelace Launched the Digital Age.* Brooklyn: Melville House, 2014.

Moore, Doris Langley. *Ada, Countess of Lovelace: Byron's Legitimate Daughter*. New York: Harper and Row, 1977.

Stein, Dorothy. *Ada: A Life and Legacy*. Cambridge: MIT Press, 1985.

Toole, Betty A., Ed.D. *Ada, The Enchantress of Numbers*. Mill Valley: Strawberry Press, 1992.

Woolley, Benjamin. *Bride of Science: Romance, Reason, and Byron's Daughter*. New York: McGraw-Hill, 1999.